CW00661994

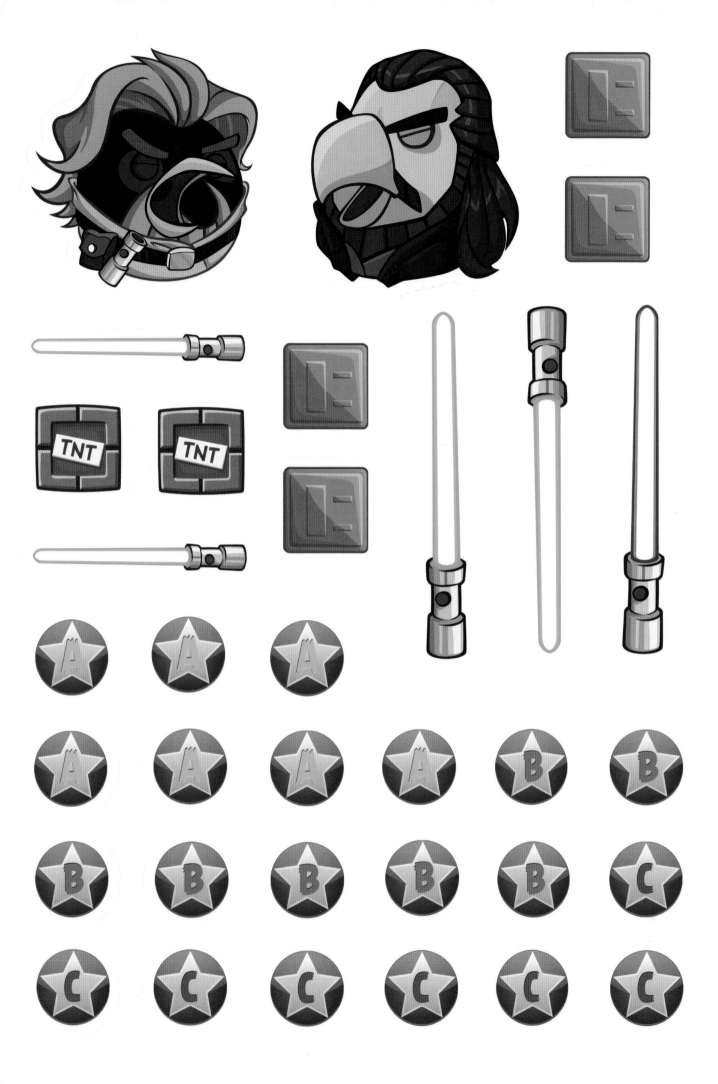

CONTENTS!

The evil Pork Federation is planning to take over the universe and steal all the sweets, treats and junk food! Only the brave Jedi Birds have a hope of stopping them.

Which side will you choose?

THE HEROES

Obi-Wan Kaboomi, Jedi Bird

Quail-Gon, Jedi Bird Master

Peckmé Amidala, Queen of Naboo

Jar Jar Wings, brave helper

Redkin Skywalker, future Jedi Bird

THE PIGGY MENACE!

All the yummy food in the universe is being stolen by the greedy Pork Federation! They've even invaded the planet Naboo to steal all their sticky buns!

Two brave Jedi Birds-Quail-Gon and young Obi-Wan Kaboomi-escape the planet with its queen Peckmé Amidala, her bodyguard Captain Namaka and a tongue-tied local called Jar Jar Wings.

Jar Jar is tongue-tied because his tongue is twice as long as he is tall!

The gang hide on the planet Tatooine where they discover the most angry bird in the universe-Redkin Skywalker! All of his anger makes Redkin very strong in the Force-in fact, he's so angry that the Jedi Bird Council's feathers are pretty ruffled when they finally meet him!

THE PORK SIDE

**DARTH SWINDLE
(EMPEROR PIGLATINE),
PIG LORD OF THE PORK SIDE**

**DARTH MOAR,
MENTAL MENACE**

**BATTLE PIGS,
WICKED WARRIORS**

**REDKIN SKYWALKER,
CORRUPTED BY THE PORK SIDE**

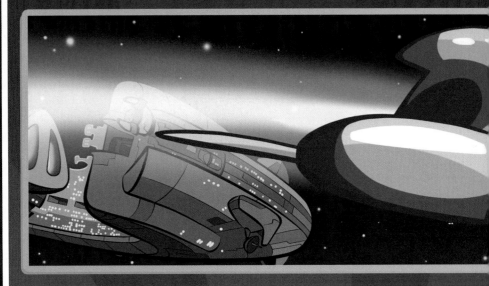

TEMPTED BY THE PORK SIDE

Quail-Gon, Obi-Wan and their allies return to Naboo to try to turn back the invaders. But a scary Lord of the Sith is waiting for them—the wicked Darth Moar. Quail-Gon battles Darth Moar in a lightsaber duel but he loses to the villain's double-bladed lightsaber (which is twice as nasty as a normal one)! Watching his friend's defeat, Obi-Wan cannot believe his eyes. He rubs them, he blinks, he even tries eye drops—but Quail-Gon is no more.

Annoyed, Obi-Wan battles Darth Moar, defeating the red-faced villain and turning back the Pork invasion.

Obi-Wan trains young Redkin to be the greatest Jedi Bird ever. But Redkin is an impatient pupil who suspects that the Jedi Birds are scared of his Jedi talent.

Redkin's anger draws him to Darth Swindle, the mysterious, black-hearted leader of the Pork forces. Darth Swindle always wears black because it hides all the stains where he's dropped food down himself and also covers up his fat belly-black is very slimming! Darth Swindle offers Redkin a shortcut to delicious food beyond his wildest dreams.

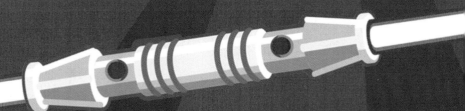

Can Redkin resist the temptation of scoffing his face?

THE HEROES

REDKIN SKYWALKER is an impatient warrior, just like Red Skywalker.

OBI-WAN KABOOMI was once a young Jedi Bird.

PECKMÉ AMIDALA is as fearless as Princess Stella.

RED SKYWALKER

OBI-WAN KABOOMI

PRINCESS STELLA ORGANA

The evil Pork Federation plans to steal all the junk food in the universe.

Only a small band of brave heroes stand in their way. Use your best hero stickers to find out

who they are—and how they line up against the classic heroes from Angry Birds "Star Wars" !

C-3PYOLK starts off without his golden plating!

R2-EGG2 is as trusty as ever! (still the secret hidden Egg)

JAR JAR WINGS is an alien sidekick-like Terebacca.

C-3PYOLK

R2-EGG2

TEREBACCA

WANTED!

REDKIN SKYWALKER

REDKIN SKYWALKER: JEDI BIRD IN TRAINING.

This young and very talented bird is training to be a Jedi under the guidance of Obi-Wan Kaboomi.

Redkin wants to know everything about the Egg, his impetuousness may prove to be his downfall.

REDKIN HAS A SECRET CRUSH ON:

ADD YOUR STICKER TO ANSWER!

WANTED!

OBI-WAN KABOOMI & JAR-JAR WINGS

OBI-WAN KABOOMI: JEDI BIRD WARRIOR.

A reliable warrior who is proud of his abilities, Kaboomi is training young Redkin in the ways of the Force.

Be warned that this fugitive has the ability to explode at will and he hasn't quite learned how to control it yet.

JAR-JAR WINGS: NOBLE-HEARTED BUT CLUMSY.

Goofy but good-natured, it's easy to underestimate Jar-Jar Wings by his appearance. Jar-Jar has a long tongue that can make junk food, and enemies disappear in the blink of an eye. He should be approached with caution.

OBI-WAN'S TEACHER WAS:

ADD YOUR STICKER TO ANSWER!

WANTED!

PECKMÉ AMIDALA & CAPTAIN NAMAKA

PECKMÉ AMIDALA: NOBLE QUEEN TURNED WARRIOR.

She may seem graceful and sweet, but Peckmé is one feisty bird when the chips are down.

Her special power is her charm, which can shake grounds with its gravity pull.

CAPTAIN NAMAKA: LOYAL BODYGUARD.

Peckmé's bodyguard, Captain Namaka, is super-fast, he has even been described as the quickest flyer in the universe.

His mission is clear: he has been hired to protect the queen and he has decided to do a very good job!

PECKMÉ SEES THE GOOD IN:

ADD YOUR STICKER TO ANSWER!

WANTED!

C-3PYOLK & R2-EGG2

R2-EGG2'S DROID BUDDY IS:

ADD YOUR STICKER TO ANSWER!

R2-EGG2: THE EGG IN DISGUISE!

This handy and resourceful droid hides an incredible secret: he's actually the one thing everyone in the universe is looking for (the all powerful egg)!

The Egg contains the Force, which is the power to rule the universe...or destroy it!

C-3PYOLK: PROTOCOL DROID.

This peaceful droid is an interpreter and translator.

He always tries to find diplomatic solutions to problems, and is friends with R2-EGG2.

C-3PYOLK WAS BUILT BY:

ADD YOUR STICKER TO ANSWER!

NABOO UNDER ATTACK

The Theed Palace is under attack. Use your stickers to protect Peckmé Amidala!

JAR JAR'S

BIRD-BRAINED JOKES

WHAT DO YOU CALL A
SCARED PORK SIDE LORD?
A SITHY!

WHAT DO YOU CALL A DROID
WHO CAN DO MARTIAL ARTS?
R2-KUNG-FU!

WHAT KIND OF BIRD
MAKES BREAD-BREAD?
THE DOUGH-DOUGH!

WHAT DO JEDI BIRDS
EAT FOR BREAKFAST?
TWEET-A-BIX!

HOW DO DROIDS
LEARN TO BE SHINY?
THEY GO TO
FINISHING SCHOOL!

WHAT IS A JEDI BIRD'S
FAVOURITE THEATRE
PERFORMANCE?
SWORD PLAY!

JEDI BIRD MIND TRICK!

These two pictures look the same to the weak minded...

But if you're strong in the Force you'll be able to find all six differences.

KNOCK-OUT!

CAN YOU HELP THE HEROIC JEDI BIRDS BATTLE THROUGH THE TOWERS AND BUST INTO THE ENEMY STRONGHOLD?

EXCLUSIVE
ANGRY BIRDS
STAR WARS II
STICKER
POSTER

THE JEDI BI

The Jedi Bird Council features the wisest of Jedi Birds. Together, they make decisions that could affect the whole of the universe!

YODA BIRD

The wisest member of the Jedi Bird Council, Yoda is a master of the Force.

Though he's small Yoda must never be underestimated—because he's a shockingly brilliant fighter.

ADD YOUR STICKER TO SHOW WHICH LIGHTSABER YODA BIRD USES.

RD COUNCIL

MOA WINDU

Moa Windu is incapable of flying but he more than makes up for that by being one of the best lightsaber fighters in the universe.

Moa is known for his startling insights-and he thinks there's something not quite right about young Redkin Skywalker.

ADD YOUR STICKER TO SHOW WHICH LIGHTSABER MOA WINDU USES.

QUAIL-GON

Quail-Gon's a maverick who doesn't play by the rules-but he's always ready to fight againt the pigs.

He bravely fought Darth Moar-and lost!

ADD YOUR STICKER TO SHOW WHICH LIGHTSABER QUAIL-JON USES.

THE PATH TO THE PORK SIDE

So you think you're a good guy? Try this quiz to see whether you could be tempted by the Pork Side...just like Redkin Skywalker!

1. WHICH OF THESE IS YOUR FAVOURITE TYPE OF FOOD?

A. Something healthy. Maybe salad or fruit.
B. A burger and fries...but you'll share the fries with your friends.
C. All the junk food in the universe, and no one else can have any.

2. WHAT WOULD YOU PREFER PEOPLE CALL YOU...?

A. Friend.
B. Master.
C. Darth.

3. YOU'RE ASKED TO GO TO A PLANET UNDERCOVER. WHAT DO YOU WEAR?

A. Simple robes so you'll blend into the background.
B. A dark cloak so you can hide in the shadows.
C. A black cape that makes you look really scary.

4. IS YOUR LIGHTSABER...?

A. Blue.
B. Green.
C. Red with two blades.

5. WHAT IS YOUR FAVOURITE FORCE TRICK?

A. Lifting heavy objects with your mind.
B. Making people agree to your wishes.
C. Strangling your enemies without touching them.

6. YOU PICK UP A SCAR DURING BATTLE. DO YOU THINK...?

A. It's so small that no one will notice.
B. It looks kind of cool— you look edgy!
C. You'd like more scars... and maybe a cybernetic hand, too!

7. TO SHOW YOUR DEVOTION TO YOUR CAUSE DO YOU...?

A. Quietly meditate.
B. Carefully follow the orders of your superiors.
C. Get your face tattooed with tiger stripes.

MOSTLY A'S–You're a good guy through and through. Expect your invitation to join the Jedi Bird Council any day now.

MOSTLY B'S–You have a bit of the bad boy about you but you're mostly walking the right path. Consult with Yoda Bird for some extra lessons in the Jedi way.

MOSTLY C'S–You're well on your way to becoming a Pork Lord of the Sith. It's time to make some tough lifestyle choices or you'll end up on the Pork Side!

YOU CAN ANSWER WITH YOUR PATH TO THE PORK SIDE STICKERS!

JEDI BIRD SEARCH!

The Jedi Birds below are jumbled up in this grid. Can you find them-plus, one extra word that spells out something you might see a Jedi Bird holding.

```
L O A E C B G J F C H A B G I D K Q
M I N R E D K I N D E F C D G L B U
D B G F R A O B A C F E M F A E C A
P A E H D B A I M O O B A K C Q D I
C O D A T C E L F D R C E B D A B L
R A E B D S T A Y G C N A W D P C J
E H Y O D A A C O B E A M F H O I A
K A E B A D F B X W G E C D P D E E
L D C G J I V A E H I S D F A R A G
A K A J E F B L G R A N C J N A D N
W U H E G P E C K M E A D B F C C H
Y B E D A G D I H E K G T U O E D P
K F C I L D B M O F S N I H B R M J
S G I E D J G A H B K E A J F B D C
```

WINDU
YODA
QUAIL
KABOOMI

JEDI
REDKIN
SKYWALKER
FORCE

EGG
PODRACER
PECKME
& _____

22

"MAY THE BIRDS BE WITH YOU"

EMPEROR PIGLATINE
& DARTH MOAR

EMPEROR PIGLATINE: ONE OF THE MOST CORRUPTED CREATURES IN THE UNIVERSE.

This nasty piggy fooled the birds into trusting him, but he's really a wicked Pig Lord called Darth Swindle.

Piglantine wants all the junk food in the universe, and he plans to become emperor to obtain and control it.

DARTH MOAR: SCARY PORK SIDE ENFORCER.

The determined and terrifying Darth Moar is a Pork Side master who appears unstoppable.

DARTH MOAR KILLED THE JEDI:

ADD YOUR STICKER TO ANSWER!

His weapon of choice is the double-bladed lightsaber.

GENERAL GRUNTER

GENERAL GRUNTER: METAL WAR MASTER.

General Grunter commands the battle pigs as they hunt the Jedi Birds.

He is merciless and his whole artificial body is a deadly weapon.

GENERAL GRUNTER'S NUMBER ONE ENEMY IS:

ADD YOUR STICKER TO ANSWER!

WARHOGS

WARHOGS: ELITE WARRIORS FOR THE PORK SIDE.

These Pig droids are far more dangerous than the ordinary battle pigs.

They're fast moving and lethal— even Jedi Birds are scared.

BATTLE PIGS

BATTLE PIGS: SOLDIERS FOR THE PORK SIDE.

These Pig droids are seemingly infinite in number. They fight for the Pork Side, but they're not too bright.

COUNT DODO
LARD VADER

COUNT DODO: JEDI BIRD WARRIOR TURNED BAD.

Count Dodo was once a Jedi Bird warrior but he was seduced by the Pork Side.

He believes that pigs are superior to birds.

COUNT DODO WAS TRAINED BY:

ADD YOUR STICKER TO ANSWER!

LARD VADER: TEMPTED BY THE PORK SIDE.

Once the bravest Jedi Bird, this youngster turned against his allies and joined the Pork Side as the wicked Lard Vader!

A supreme fighter, Lard Vader wants The Egg so that he can become ruler of the Universe.

Lard Vader was once Redkin Skywalker...

PIGLATINE IS LOOKING FOR A FEW GOOD PIGS!

START HERE...

DO YOU LIKE TAKING ORDERS OR GIVING THEM?

DO PEOPLE FOLLOW THE ORDERS YOU GIVE?

GIVING

TAKING

NO

ARE YOU GOOD AT REMEMBERING THINGS?

YES

ARE YOU GOOD AT COMING UP WITH PLANS?

YES

NO

NO

CAN YOU HANDLE YOURSELF WHEN UNDER STRESS?

YES

WELL DONE! YOU'RE A PIG FIELD COMMANDER.

Joining the Pork Side could not be easier–nor more rewarding. We have all the treats, all the sweets, and we wear black which is very slimming (handy when you're eating all those delicious sweets, donuts and burgers). So why not join us? You will? Good. Just fill in this personality quiz to find out your new role on the winning side!

P.S. If you want to be a Lard of the Pork Side like Darth Vader you'll need an evil name–check out your evil new name in the handy column to the right.

NOT REALLY

ALWAYS

ARE YOU HAPPY TO PUT YOUR OWN DESIRES ABOVE THOSE OF YOUR FRIENDS?

BUT WOULD YOU BE HAPPY TO MAKE THEM FOLLOW YOUR ORDERS ANYWAY?

NO

YES

YES

NO

FRIENDS?!! HAHA! I DON'T NEED FRIENDS!

WE NEED SOME CANNON FODDER. YOU'RE A PIG TROOPER!

YOU HAVE EVERYTHING IT TAKES TO BE A NEW LARD OF THE PORK SIDE!

YOUR PORK SIDE NAME:

It's easy to find your Pork Side name! You'll find your new name next to the first letter of your name in the list below. Don't forget to add "Darth" to the start!

A Nasty
B Horrid
C Smelly
D Noisy
E Stinky
F Unpleasant
G Cross-eyes
H Foul
I Meany
J Awful
K Clumsy
L Gross
M Dreadful
N Stench
O Horrendous
P Pick-a-nose
Q Beastly
R Ghastly
S Appalling
T Needing Soap
U Terrible
V Frightful
W Shocking
X Unpleasant smell
Y Annoying
Z Irritating

DROID-NAPPED!

OH MY CIRCUITS! THOSE CRAZY JAWA BIRDS ARE REPROGRAMMING STOLEN DROIDS. USE YOUR STICKERS TO SHOW THE RESULTS!

JOKES FROM THE
PORK SIDE

What medicine does Darth Moar use on his scarred face? Oinkment!

What does Piglatine wash with? Bubble darth!

Which dark lord stays warm in winter? Scarf Vader!

What do battle pigs use to communicate? Walkie-porkies.

Why did the battle pig want an extra nose? So he couldn't be snoutnumbered!

Why did Redkin Skywalker go to the pig playground? Because he was drawn to the Pork Slide!

REDKIN GOOD, REDKIN BAD!

COLOUR THIS PAGE TO SEE REDKIN'S TRANSFORMATION TO THE PORK SIDE.

PODRACER

PADAWAN

SITH APPRENTICE

MAKE YOUR OWN

YOU WILL NEED:

1. The cardboard core from an empty toilet roll.

2. The cardboard core from an empty kitchen roll.

3. Some brightly coloured wrapping paper or foil.

4. Scissors (ask an adult to help).

5. Paper glue and sticky tape.

6. A pen or pencil.

7. Pork Side cunning!

INSTRUCTIONS:

1. To make Lard Vader's lightsaber, start by taking the toilet roll core. This will be the handle.

2. Decorate the toilet roll core by wrapping it in silver foil to make it look like metal. Tuck the foil in and trim it using the scissors. You may also need to glue it in place.

3. Next add some stickers for the handle's switches of your lightsaber.

4. Now take the kitchen roll core. This will be the blade of your lightsaber.

5. Wrap the kitchen roll core in patterned paper. You can find shiny wrapping paper in lots of different shades-red is perfect for a Lard of the Pork Side but you could use any colour so long as it's bright.

6. Just like the handle, you'll need to trim the wrapping to fit and may require some glue to fix it in place.

TOP TIP: To make a double-bladed lightsaber like Darth Moar's, simply follow the same process but use two kitchen roll cores for the blades, slotting these in place-one at each end.

LIGHTSABER

EVERY PORK LORD AND JEDI BIRD NEEDS A LIGHTSABER, AND YOU CAN MAKE ONE AT HOME.

TIP: Leave a little space at the bottom uncovered to make it easier to connect to the handle.

7. Now you need to slot the blade into the handle. This may take a little effort—a useful trick is to make a cut of 1-2 centimetres down the top of the handle so that it opens out a little, and if you make a similar cut to the base of your blade, that allows it to crunch in on itself enough to slip inside. (If that's not enough, try two cuts on each handle!)

8. A little sticky tape or glue will fix the blade to the handle if needed.

9. You now have a lightsaber worthy of a Dark Lard of the Pork Side.

WARNING!!! SCISSORS ARE SHARP! ALWAYS ASK FOR HELP FROM AN ADULT!

GALACTIC TRANSMISSION

PORK SIDE FORCES ARE AMASSING IN CONTESTED SPACE.
ADD YOUR STICKERS TO SHOW THE MIGHT OF THE BAD GUYS!

TRANSMISSION END

EXCLUSIVE
ANGRY BIRDS
STAR WARS
II
STICKER
POSTER

ESCAPE FROM THE PORK SIDE

Here's a great game to play with a friend. You can be the hero trying to reach The Egg, or you might be the bad guy who must stop the hero!

You will need:

- Two players
- Two counters: which you can make from your stickers.
- 1 dice

How to play:

1. First, place the Hero Counter on the Hero Start and the Bad Guy Counter on the Pork Side Start.

2. Both players roll the dice to see who will play who. The Hero is the player who rolls the highest number. If you get the same number, just roll again.

3. The Hero moves first, take turns after this.

4. Both players must follow the instructions on any space that they land on.

5. The bad guy rolls again whenever they land on a red space!

The object of the game:

Both players are trying to reach the Egg. However, the bad guy can also win by landing on the Hero and capturing the Hero for the Pork Side.

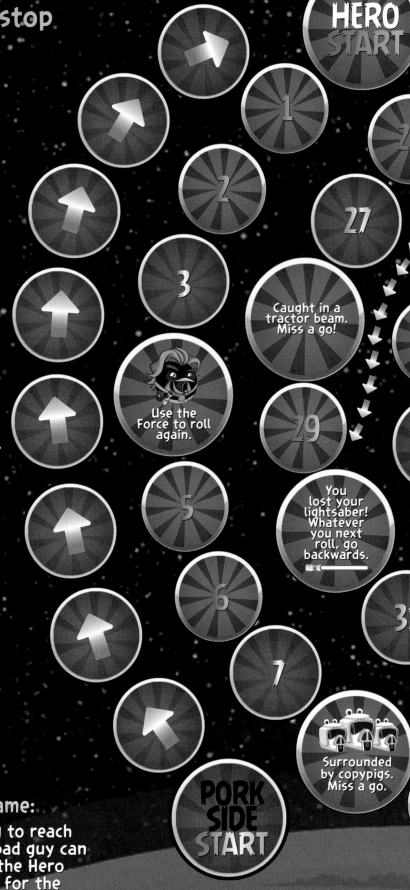

HERO START

1

28

2

27

3

Caught in a tractor beam. Miss a go!

Use the Force to roll again.

29

5

You lost your lightsaber! Whatever you next roll, go backwards.

6

31

7

Surrounded by copypigs. Miss a go.

PORK SIDE START

40

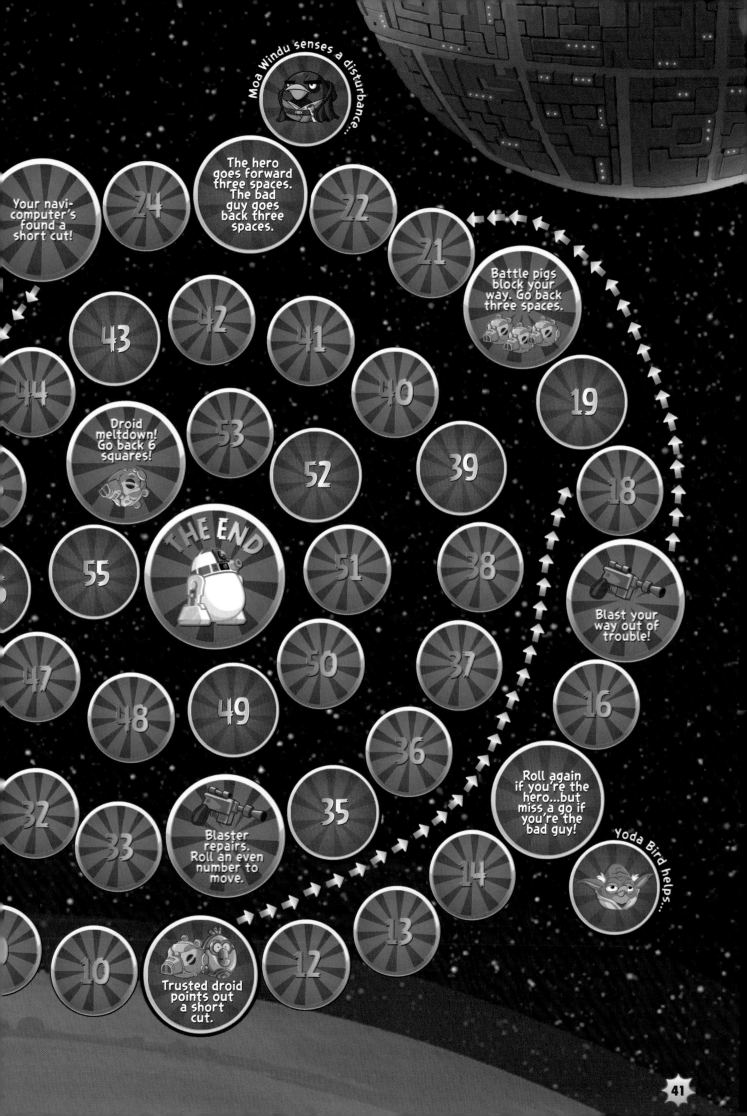

Moa Windu senses a disturbance...

Your navi-computer's found a short cut!

24

The hero goes forward three spaces. The bad guy goes back three spaces.

22

21

Battle pigs block your way. Go back three spaces.

43

42

41

40

19

44

Droid meltdown! Go back 6 squares!

53

52

39

18

55

THE END

51

38

Blast your way out of trouble!

47

50

37

16

48

49

36

Roll again if you're the hero...but miss a go if you're the bad guy!

32

33

Blaster repairs. Roll an even number to move.

35

14

Yoda Bird helps...

10

Trusted droid points out a short cut.

12

13

DISGUISED AS BATTLE PIGS!

PORK SIDE FORCES HAVE INVADED THE PEACEFUL PLANET OF NABOO.

BUT COULD SOME VALIANT HEROES HAVE SNUCK INTO THEIR SINISTER RANKS?

SEE IF YOU CAN FIND...

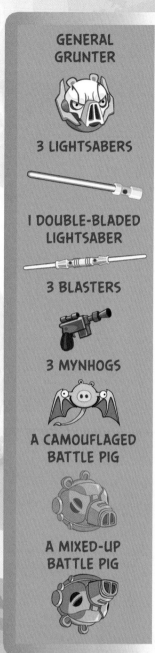

GENERAL GRUNTER

3 LIGHTSABERS

1 DOUBLE-BLADED LIGHTSABER

3 BLASTERS

3 MYNHOGS

A CAMOUFLAGED BATTLE PIG

A MIXED-UP BATTLE PIG

OBI-WAN KABOOMI

MOA WINDU

YODA BIRD

JAR JAR WINGS

PECKMÉ AMIDALA

C-3PYOLK

R2-EGG2

CAPTAIN NAMAKA

THE BOUNTY HUNTERS!

Bounty hunters are really mean and will work for whoever pays them! Add a splash of colour to their armour and maybe they won't come after you!

A mockingbird who can transform her appearance at will!

JANGO FATT

ZAM WEASEL

Armed with a jetpack to get him out of trouble, Jango hunts hero birds if the price is right!

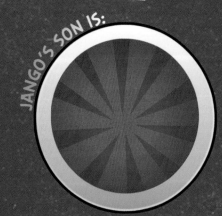

JANGO'S SON IS:

ZAM WEASEL'S WEAPON OF CHOICE IS:

DESIGN YOUR OWN
BOUNTY HUNTER!

Now you're calling the shots! Use your pens, pencils and stickers to invent a really cool bounty hunter. They might even join the heroic Jedi Birds in battling the Pork Side!

HEROES VS VILLAINS

The call has gone out! Familiar faces appear for the final battle. Use your stickers to decide who wins—or loses!

EXCLUSIVE
ANGRY BIRDS
STAR WARS
II
STICKER
POSTER

ANSWERS!

PAGE 08 - WANTED:
REDKIN SKYWALKER
Redkin has a secret
crush on Peckmé
Amidala.

PAGE 09 - WANTED: OBI-WAN
KABOOMI
Obi-Wan's teacher
was Quail-Gon.

PAGE 10 - WANTED: PECKMÉ
AMIDALA
Peckmé sees the good
in Redkin Skywalker.

PAGE 11 - WANTED: C-3PYOLK
& R2-EGG2
C-3PYolk was built by
Redkin Skywalker.
R2-EGG2's droid buddy
is C-3PYOLK.

PAGE 15 - JEDI BIRD MIND TRICK!

PAGE 42 -

PAGE 18 - THE JEDI BIRD COUNCIL
Yoda and Quail-Gon
use a green lightsaber.
Moa uses a purple
lightsaber.

PAGE 22 - JEDI BIRD SEARCH!

PAGE 27 - PIGLATINE &
DARTH MOAR
Darth Moar killed the
Jedi Quail-Gon.

PAGE 28 - GENERAL GRUNTER
General Grunter's
number one enemy is
Obi-Wan Kaboomi.

PAGE 29 - COUNT DODO
Count Dodo was
trained by Yoda Bird

PAGE 44 - THE BOUNTY HUNTERS!
Jango's son is
Boba Fatt.
Zam Weasel's weapon
of choice is a blaster.